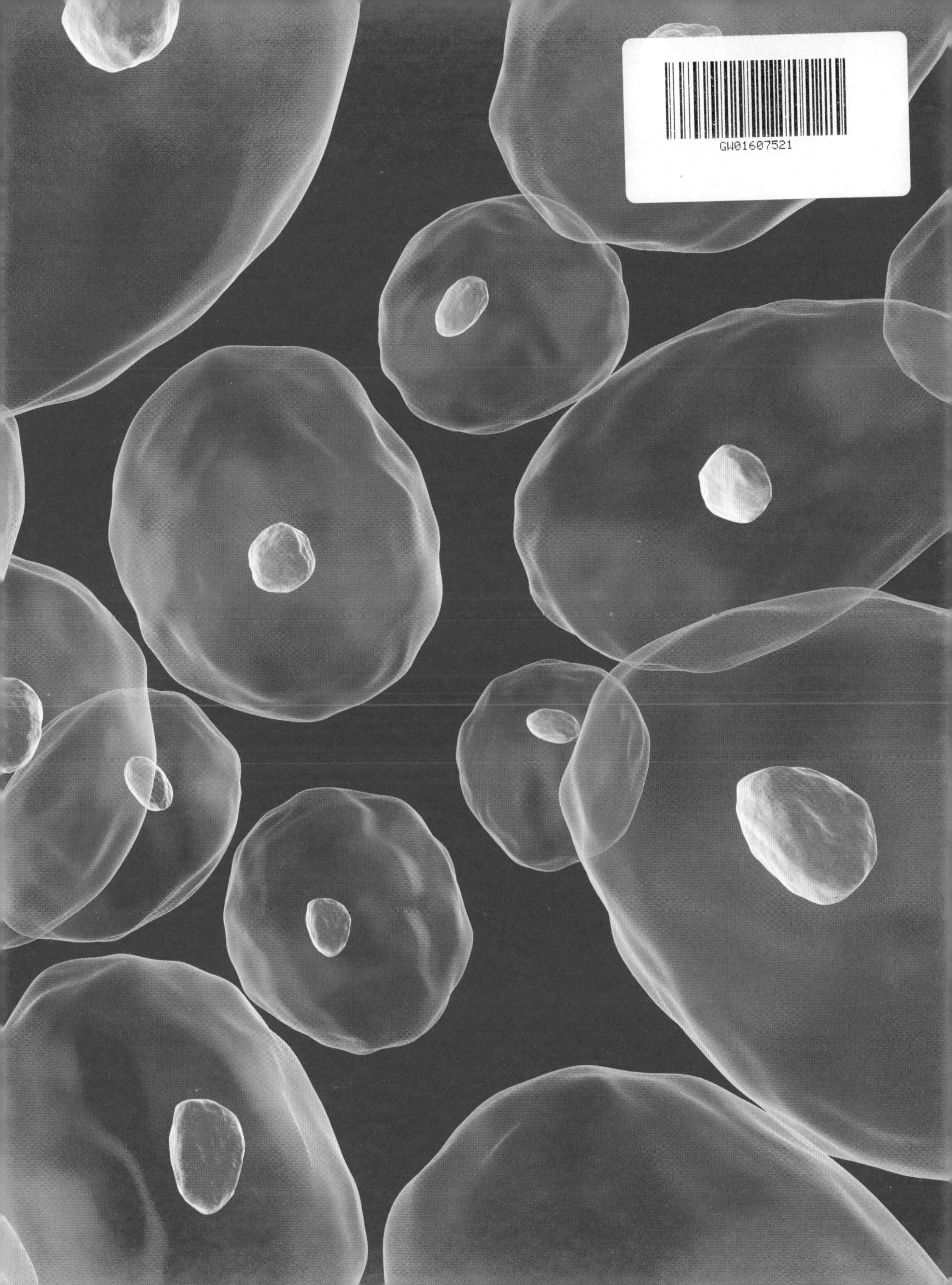
GW01607521

How to Make a Human

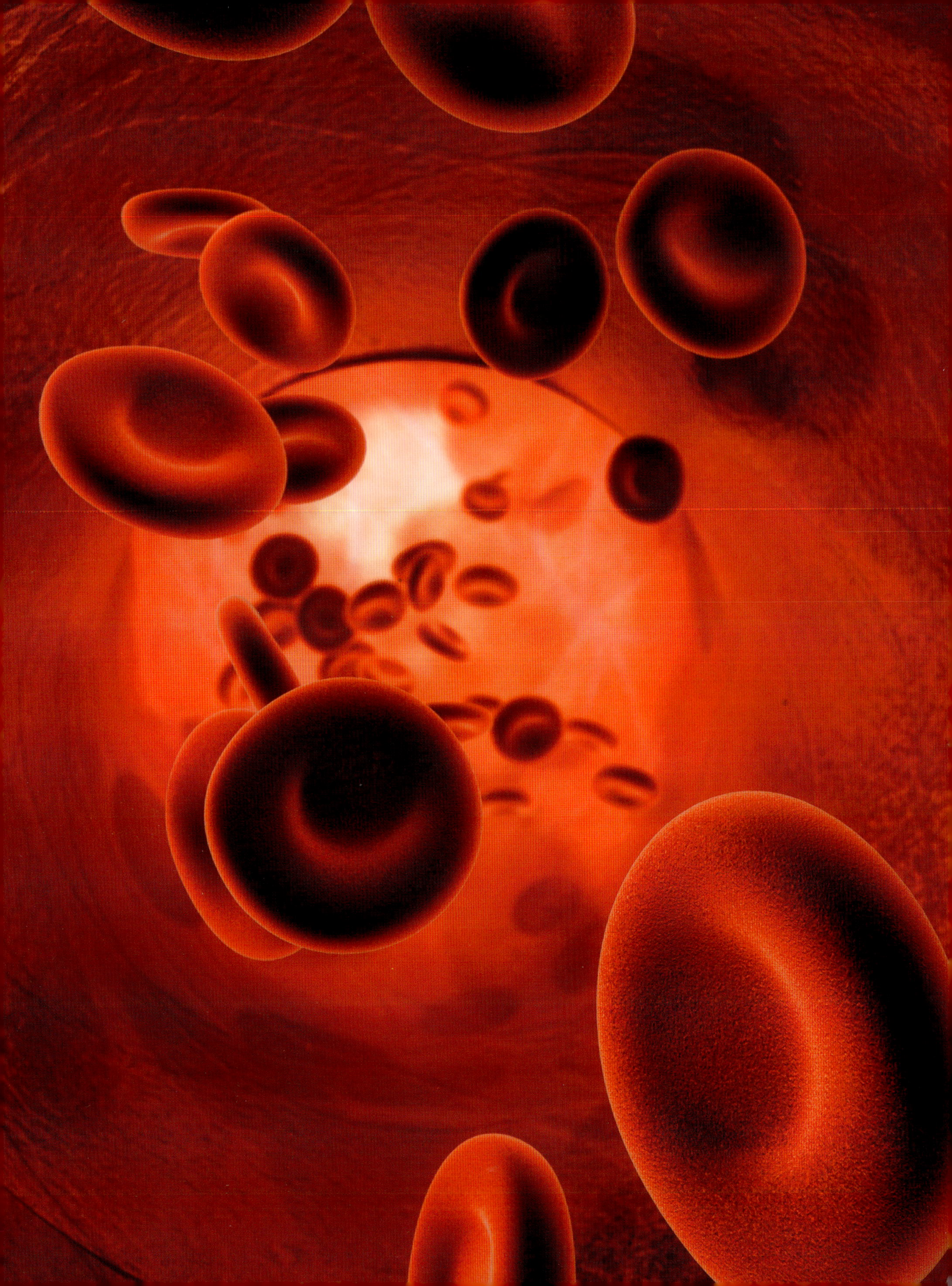

How to Make a Human

What if you could build a human from scratch?

Written by Scott Forbes   Idea by Ariana Klepac

WeldonOwen
PUBLISHING

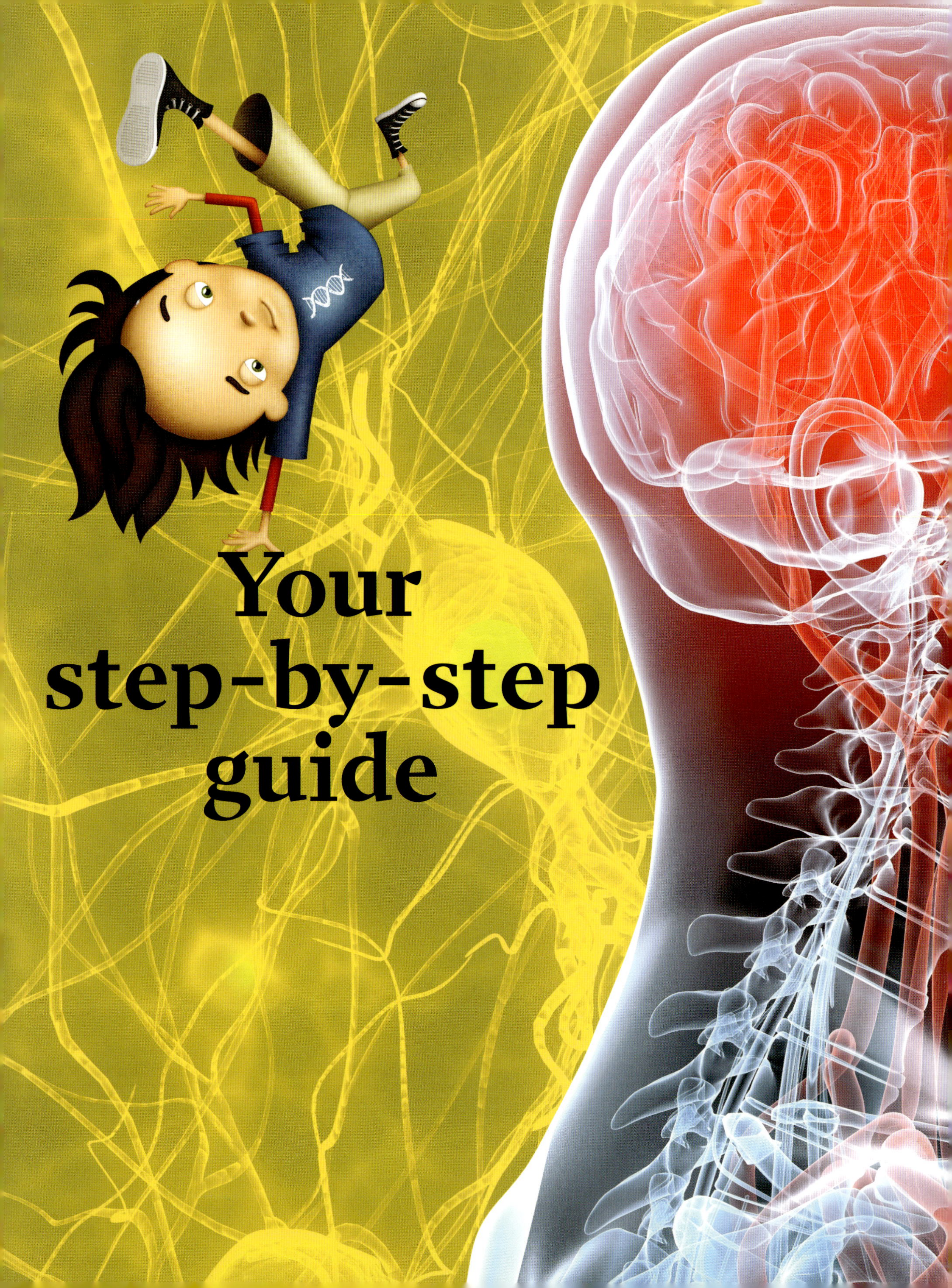

Your step-by-step guide

So, You Want to Make a Human?

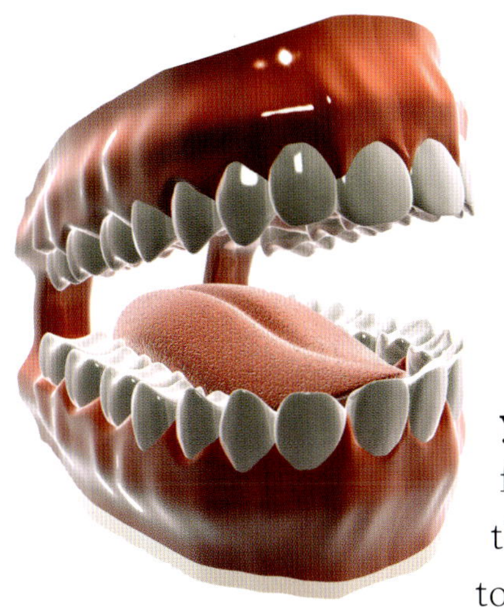

OK! What's the best way to understand something complex or technical? Take it apart, or make it yourself. Suppose you could build a human from scratch. Imagine you could order all the pieces you need and have them delivered to your door. And then you could fit them all together to make a living, breathing, brainy human just like you. It would be fun, wouldn't it? It would be complicated, of course, and rather fiddly – and no doubt a bit messy. But you'd learn a huge amount about yourself, and other humans, along the way.

Well, this book is going to show you what that would be like. It contains all the advice, information and instructions you'll need to make a human body, and guides you through every phase of construction. As you piece a human together, you'll find out how every part of your body operates – how you think, see, taste and feel, how you breathe, eat, smile and sing. And you'll realise how amazing a human is – a tough and astonishingly efficient machine and the most intelligent life form known ever, anywhere. Yes, that's you!

So, to find out just how amazing you really are, read on!

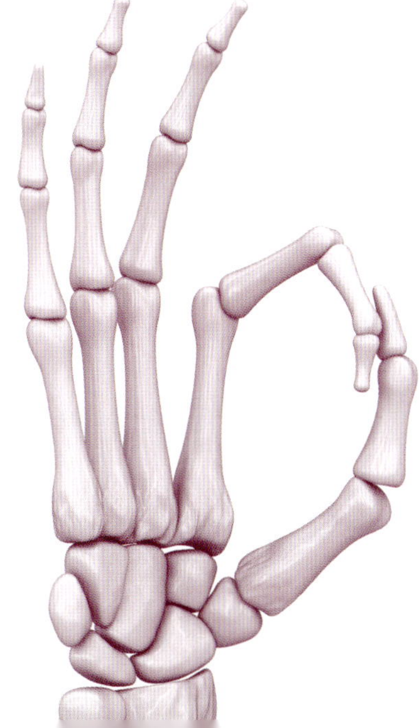

The Body Kit

CHECK IT OUT Before you start making your human, make sure you have all the parts you need. There's nothing more frustrating than getting to the end of a puzzle and finding that one piece is missing.

TAKE A LOOK So, what do you need to make a body? Well, have a look at yourself. There's that lovely covering of skin of course, and quite a bit of hair. You've got a head, arms and legs, fingers and toes, eyes, ears, a nose and a mouth. Under the skin are those muscles you use to run, jump, dance, skateboard, lift huge weights and fly (well, maybe not all those things). There's a bit of fat here and there (you still look great though) and lots of harder,

knobbly bits that stick out through the muscles – the bones, of course.

Deeper inside are the organs: the lungs that suck in air, the heart that pumps life-giving blood and oxygen around your body, the stomach that processes all that food you eat. And, not least, the brain you are now using to read and understand these words. Wow, you're quite a package!

Start Small

Weird as it may seem, all these bits and pieces – and you – began as a single cell; a microscopic parcel of chemicals smaller than the dot on this i. This cell was able to perform the clever trick of dividing itself in two, a process called mitosis. Then those two cells divided themselves, and the resulting four split in two, and so on, until there were hundreds, then thousands, then millions of them.

Cell

All this got under way before you were born, and since then it has never stopped. You've grown and grown, and now you have at least 75 *trillion* cells – that's 75 million million or 75,000,000,000,000. Awesome!

The Cell Factory

Each cell contains a range of substances, including oxygen, carbon, hydrogen, nitrogen and calcium, which come from the food you eat. Cells turn these substances into chemicals that a body needs to function.

At the centre of most cells is the nucleus, which controls operations. Around it, contained in a jelly-like mass known as the cytoplasm, are components called organelles, each of which has a specific job to do – gathering nutrients, turning them into energy, getting rid of waste. As you'll see, that's a bit like your body in miniature!

Every day, you produce 300 billion new cells!

TEAMING UP Cells develop into different types. Cells of the same type then team up in huge numbers to form what are known as tissues, which in turn combine to make muscles, organs and other body parts.

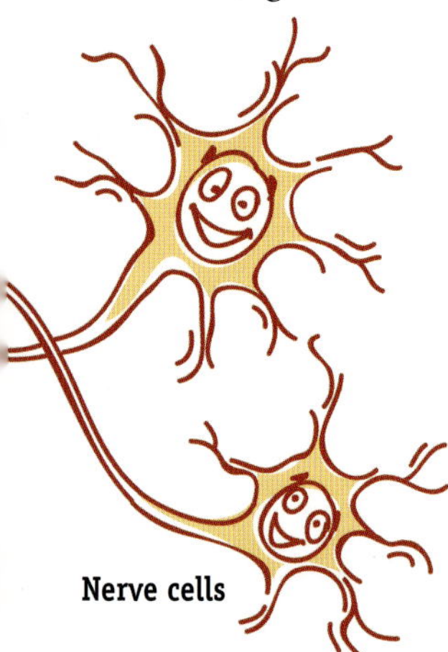

Nerve cells

To make a fully functioning human, you need about 200 kinds of cells, including blood, muscle, fat, nerve and skin cells. If you peered at these cells through a microscope, you would see that they all look different. Nerve cells, for example, have tentacle-like parts that connect them to other nerve cells. Muscle cells are long and stretchy. Fat cells are round and, well, fat.

COMING AND GOING These types of cells all have different life spans. Skin cells, for instance, divide to make new cells every day. That's just as well, as otherwise, with all the wear and tear you subject it to, your skin might soon be full of holes. Most of your brain cells, on the other hand, stay alive as long as you do – which is fortunate, as that helps you remember who you are, what you have done, and what you were planning to do after reading this.

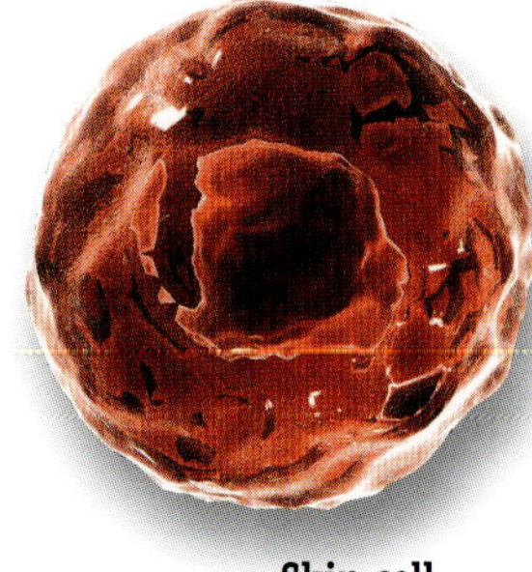

Skin cell

Everyone's DNA is slightly different. Scientists can now match the tiniest traces of DNA – such as skin flakes and specks of saliva – to their owner.

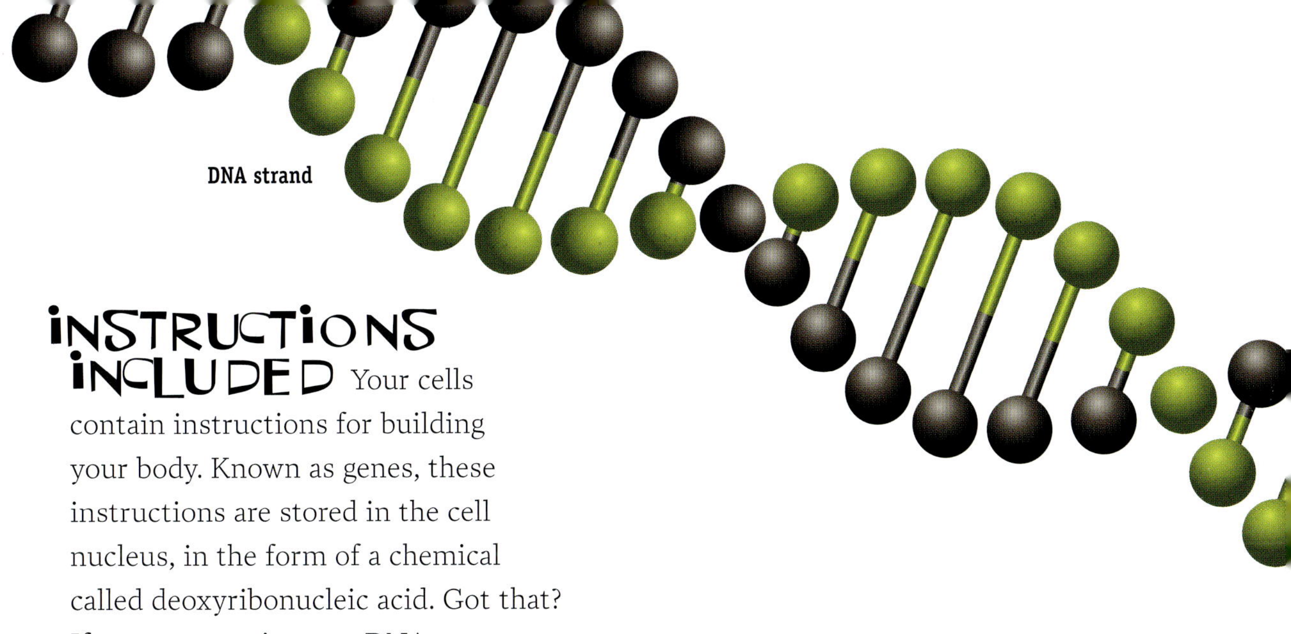

INSTRUCTIONS INCLUDED

Your cells contain instructions for building your body. Known as genes, these instructions are stored in the cell nucleus, in the form of a chemical called deoxyribonucleic acid. Got that? If not, you can just say DNA.

DNA is a long molecule that wraps itself into a tiny bundle called a chromosome — a microscopic instruction booklet. Each human cell has 46 chromosomes; 23 of them are copies of chromosomes from your mum and 23 are copies of chromosomes from your dad. Other creatures have different numbers of chromosomes, but having more doesn't necessarily make you any smarter. Your cat might

Chromosome

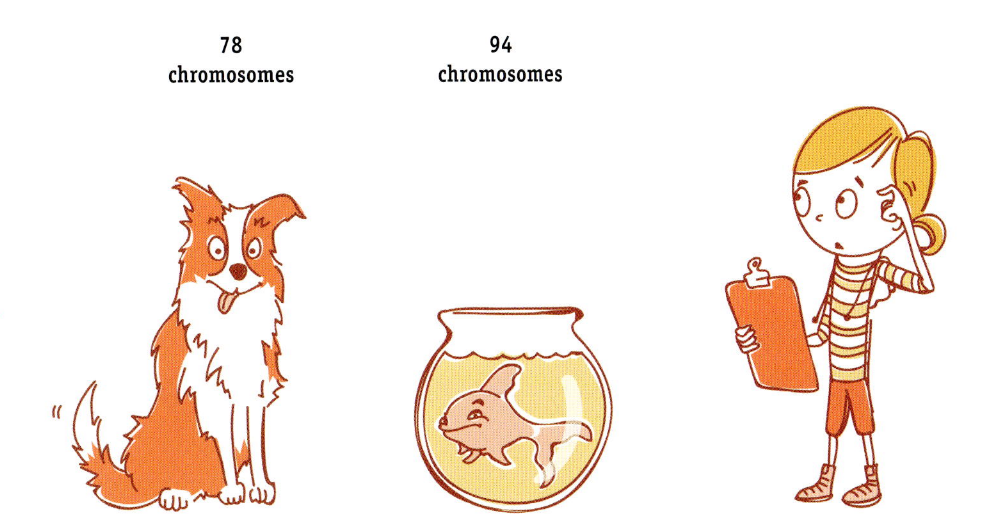

Build a Framework

BARE BONES As with any large structure, a human body needs a superstrong framework, so the first thing to do is build the skeleton.

Pick up one of the long bones. Hard and strong, isn't it? But perhaps not as heavy as you thought? That's because it isn't completely solid. The thick, outer layer, called compact bone, is tough – the hardest substance in your body after your tooth enamel. But inside is a light honeycomb-like structure of struts and holes known as spongy bone, and at the centre of a long bone is a narrow cavity.

Blood cells

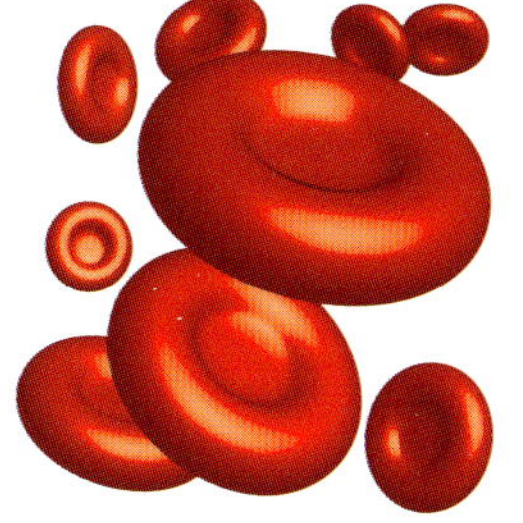

Though we tend to think of bones as lifeless, the holes in a functioning bone are full of blood vessels and the cavity contains a soft, squishy substance called bone marrow. It's this marrow that makes your blood cells – at the rate of over 2 million every second.

Err, hang on. That doesn't look right.

PROVIDE BACKUP

Begin by assembling the body's central support, the spine, or backbone. It consists of 26 strangely shaped bones called vertebrae, which are stacked one on top of the other to form a long, curving column. This arrangement might look a little unsteady, but it's strong enough to support that heavy head of yours. It's also extremely flexible, allowing you to bend and turn in every direction. And master some supercool dance moves.

TAIL AND TOP

Start at the tail. What, you didn't know you had a tail? Yep, you do. Called your coccyx, it's a tiny bone at the very bottom of your spine. It's all that's left of a longer tail that human ancestors possessed millions of years ago.

Spine

Coccyx

The coccyx is at the bottom of the sacrum, a large triangular bone. On top of the sacrum you'll need to stack the five widest vertebrae, the lumbar vertebrae, which support most of your weight. Above that, attach the next 12, the thoracic vertebrae, and join them to the ribs. There are 12 pairs of ribs, which curve together to form the rib cage, which protects your most vital organs. Make sure it's at the front!

On top of the thoracic ribs, place the seven smallest vertebrae, known as the cervical vertebrae. These allow the neck to move freely. Got that? If so, just flex your top vertebrae – and nod.

HIP, HIP! The sacrum is joined to the hips, two large, flat bones on either side of it, and together these bones make up the pelvis. The pelvis transfers the weight of the upper body from the spine to the feet.

Pelvis

Now look for the two longest bones in your kit. These are the thighbones, or femurs. The ball at the top slots into

Meeting Points

Your body has around 400 joints – places where bones connect. Some barely move, but others are very flexible. So-called pivot joints, like the ones in your neck, enable bones to rotate. Hinge joints such as the knee allow bones to swing only one way. Ball-and-socket joints like the hips provide the most movement. Most joints are reinforced with bands of stretchy tissue called ligaments.

a socket on the underside of the hip. This so-called ball-and-socket joint allows the thigh to move freely in most directions. If your muscles are flexible enough, it will even let you do splits. Go on, give it a try!

STEADY AS YOU GO

The legs consist of two major sections, the femur at the top and a pair of long bones, the tibia and fibula, at the bottom. These are connected by the largest joint in your body, the knee, which is protected by an extra little bone at the front, the kneecap or patella. As you may have noticed, the knee joint bends only one way and locks when straight. If it moved in other directions too, you'd be wobbling about and using far more energy just to stay upright!

FANCY FOOTWORK

It's been fairly easy so far, don't you think? But now you've got your work cut out for you. Because each foot contains no fewer than 26 bones!

At the back is a group of seven blocky bones, the tarsals, including the ankle bone and heel bone. Five long thin bones, the metatarsals, link these to the five toes, which have 14 separate bones (called phalanges) – two in each of the big toes and three in each of the others. Phew!

A FIRM BASE Does a foot really have to be so complicated, you might say? Well, all these little bones help us make constant tiny movements that keep us balanced. So it's worth taking the trouble to get this right. But when you've finished, you might just want to, er, put your feet up.

Your hands and feet contain more than half of all your bones.

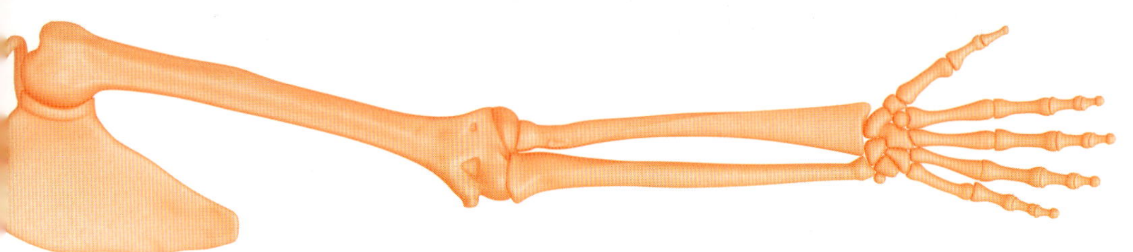

ARM 'N' ARM

After building the legs, the arms should be a breeze. The two sets of limbs have a lot in common, after all. You've got wide flat bones at the top, the shoulder blades (which are joined to the rib cage by the collar bones), and another pair of ball-and-socket joints that connect the arms to the shoulder blades. The arms too have a long upper bone, the humerus, and a double lower bone, consisting of the radius and the ulna. And these two sections meet at the elbow, which, like the knee, is a hinge joint.

PUT YOUR HANDS TOGETHER

So, the arms: easy, aren't they? But then you get to the hands and guess what: yep, it's like the feet all over again. Lots of little bones – 27 this time. Start with the wrist. You might think it would be one bone, but no, it's made up of eight knobbly bones called carpals. Five long bones, the metacarpals, link these to the fingers (each of which has three bones, or phalanges) and the thumb (two bones).

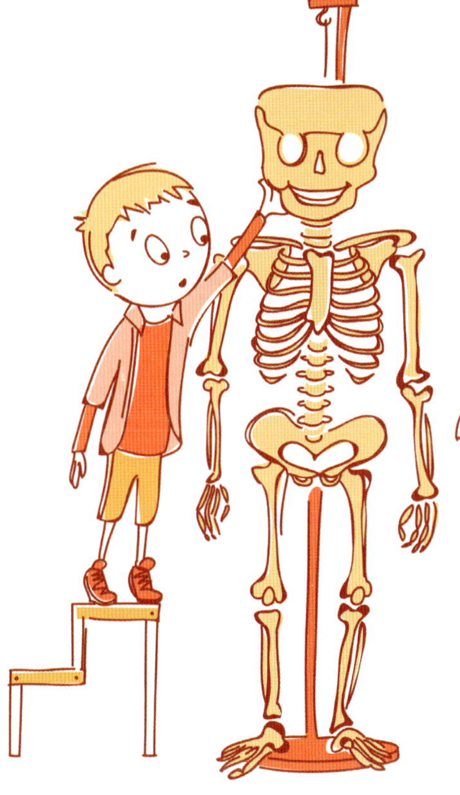

Your skeleton is complete. If you've been keeping count, you'll know there are 206 bones in total. As a baby, you have about 270, but some join together as you grow.

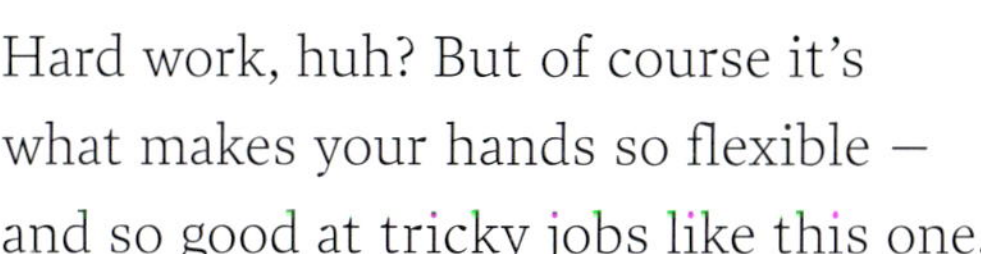

Hard work, huh? But of course it's what makes your hands so flexible – and so good at tricky jobs like this one.

HEADS UP At least making the hands and feet is good preparation for the skull. It has 28 bones, and they are all odd shapes and sizes and have to be slotted together like jigsaw pieces. Start with the 14 bones that make up the face. These include the only one in the skull that moves, the lower jaw or mandible. Just as well it does, otherwise eating and speaking would be seriously challenging.

Finally, assemble the six small ear bones and the eight bones of the cranium, the top of the skull. Then get ready to seal the skull and place it on the top vertebra. But wait: just before you do that, we need to insert something vital – the most important thing of all ...

FUNNY – NOT!

The elbow is the location of the funny bone. If you have ever bumped yours hard, you'll know that's the worst name ever for a body part. It's not even a bone, for goodness sake, but a type of nerve. The name is thought to come from the word humerus, the name of the upper arm bone. Humorous, get it? Hmm.

step 3

Install the Control Centre

Think about it

A human can't think, move or make sense of the world without a brain. So that's the first organ you'll need to add. Place it in the skull then prepare to wire it to the rest of the body.

THE BRAIN A big wrinkled blob of grey jelly, the brain doesn't exactly look lively. But it can store far more information and work far faster than any computer. The three main parts you can see are: the large cerebrum on top; the small cerebellum underneath, which helps with balance; and, next to it, the brain stem.

That wrinkled, outer part of the cerebrum is called the cerebral cortex.

You'll notice that a deep groove divides it into two halves, or hemispheres. The left one controls and receives information from the right-hand side of the body; the right hemisphere controls and receives information from the left side of the body.

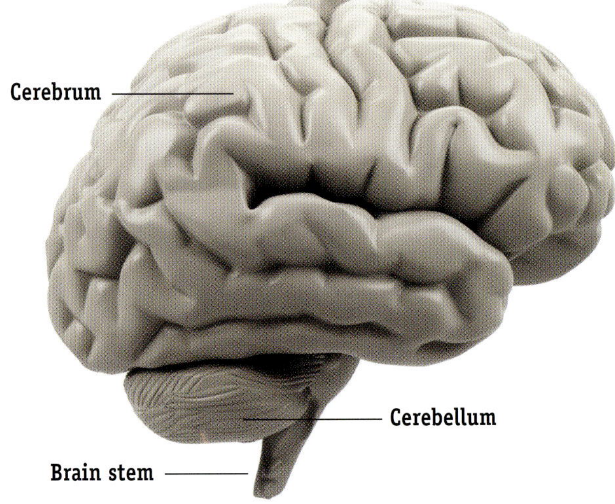

Particular parts of each hemisphere control certain abilities, such as speech, maths, language, and recognising faces and other things. An area at the back of the cortex deals with vision, while the big bulging front part is where we do most of our thinking and decision-making.

Hot-Wired

Each nerve carries several long cells called neurones, which transmit messages as electrical impulses. There are two main kinds of nerves. Sensory nerves relay messages to the brain about the outside world, including sensations such as heat and pain. Motor nerves carry messages from the brain telling your body what to do. Thousands of messages reach and leave the brain every second.

A BUNDLE OF NERVES The brain's link to the rest of the body is the spinal cord, a thick bundle of nerves. Connect this main cable to the brain stem and run it down through the inside of the backbone. Together, the brain and spinal cord are known as the central nervous system.

Next, you'll need to hook up the hundreds of smaller cables, called nerves, which run from the backbone to the rest of the body. A human has about 70 km of these, so this could take some time.

Free nerve endings sense heat, and help you to enjoy a lovely hot bath.

GET IN TOUCH

The nerves will eventually be connected to the skin, which contains several kinds of nerve endings. Some, called receptors, register pressure and stretching. Others, called free nerve endings, sense heat, cold and pain.

Make sure you extend the nerves to all parts of the body, especially the eyes, mouth and fingers. After all, these parts tell you heaps about the outside world. Your fingers, for example, can feel the softest touches and the tiniest differences in texture.

EARLY WARNING

Messages from these body parts can be lightning fast, travelling at up to 100 m a second or 360 km an hour. Touch a hot stove for example – aargh! – and you'll snatch back your hand and leap into the air before you even realise what's happened. Reactions like this are called reflexes.

EYE, EYE Okay, next the eyes. Yes, they are round and rubbery, but please don't bounce them. Pop them into the sockets in the skull, or orbits as they are also known. Six straps of muscle attach each eyeball to the sockets and make the eyes move. An optic nerve connects each eye to the brain.

At the front of the eye, the coloured iris surrounds the black pupil. Both are covered by a thin clear layer called the cornea. Behind them is the lens of the eye, and inside the back of the eye is a highly sensitive area called the retina.

The Long and Short of It

If your eyeball is too long, light from the lens will focus in front of the retina. That makes you short-sighted, and you'll have trouble seeing things far away. If your eyeball is too short, the light will be focused beyond the retina, in which case you'll be long-sighted and maybe struggle to make out the words on this page. Either way, you'll need glasses.

LOOK OUT When you look at something, light enters the eye through the pupil. The lens focuses the pattern of light onto the retina, which translates it into signals that whizz along the optic nerve to the brain. The brain then compares the information from the two eyes to create a moving 3D image.

HEAR, HEAR

What you call your ears – those flaps on the side of your head – are simply folds of cartilage and skin that direct sounds into your skull (you'll add them later). The tricky work of hearing is carried out inside the skull, by a cluster of nerves, the three tiniest bones in your body, and a drum.

BEAT THE DRUM

Yep, a drum. Sounds travel through the air as pressure waves, and on their way down your earhole, or ear canal, they strike a thin sheet of skin – the eardrum. On the other side of this skin, in what's known as the inner ear, are the three tiny bones, the ossicles – named the malleus (meaning hammer), incus (anvil) and stapes (stirrup) after their shapes. Let's hope you remembered to put them in because their role is vital!

The sound waves make the eardrum vibrate, which in turn moves the tiny bones. This creates pressure waves in the inner ear that are sensed by a coiled nerve called the cochlea. It converts the waves to nerve messages, which the brain recognises as sounds. Oh no, not *that* song again!

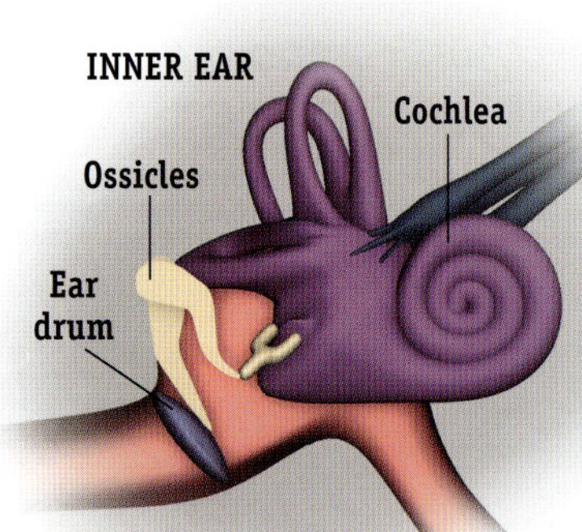

Not only does your dog have more chromosomes than you, it can also hear much better. Dogs sense very high-pitched sounds that we don't even notice.

If the air pressure on either side of the eardrum is not balanced, your hearing may become muffled. A tube linking the inner ear with the throat and nose – the Eustachian tube – can, however, let air in and out. So by swallowing, yawning or blowing your nose you can often fix this problem. This is called 'making your ears pop'.

GO FOR A SPIN Quickly spin yourself around. Then do it again. And again. Dizzy yet? Stand still for a minute. Still dizzy? When you spin, fluid in tubes inside your inner ear, known as the semicircular canals, starts swirling too. This movement makes you feel dizzy. And even after you stop, the fluid keeps moving. So it takes a little while for the dizziness to pass.

RIGHT WAY UP?

Along with visual images and muscle and touch sensations, the movement of these inner ear fluids also tells your brain whether you are upright, tilted at an angle or even upside down. In response, the brain adjusts your body to keep you balanced. Or it suggests that you get your feet back on the ground at once.

MATTERS OF TASTE

Make sure you have hooked up the nerves in the nose and mouth too. Otherwise your human will show absolutely no appreciation for your cooking. The main smell sensors, or olfactory bulbs, sit behind the top of your nose, just under the front of the brain. The taste sensors, or gustatory nerves, are arranged around the mouth, throat and tongue.

MMM OR EUGHH?

When you breathe in, your nose draws in scent molecules from whatever is in the air. The molecules dissolve in the mucus at the top of your nose and activate smell cells, which send messages via the olfactory nerves to the brain. That's when you find out if it's a good smell or a bad one. Mmm, or eughh?

Taste cells line your tongue, mouth and throat and pass messages to the gustatory nerves. They can identify a huge range of flavours, which are often divided into five main tastes: sweet, sour, bitter, salty and savoury. Which do you prefer?

Taste buds die out as you get older, so your sense of taste is keener than your parents'. Your dog wins out on the smelling front though: while humans have about 5 million smell receptors in their noses, dogs have about 200 million and can distinguish far more scents.

DYNAMIC DUO

Smell and taste are a double act. They work together to alert you to things that might be harmful, such as foods that have gone off. While we tend to think taste is the stronger sense, much of what we think we taste we actually smell. If you're not convinced, try holding your nose when you eat a favourite food. Doesn't taste quite so good now, does it?

CONSTANT WATCH

Other parts of your body also help your brain monitor vital processes and react to the outside world. Small organs called glands produce chemicals known as hormones that help to keep all your body systems in balance, and some are triggered by things you sense. For example, a scary sight – someone coming towards you on a skateboard, totally out of control – causes your adrenal glands in the abdomen to make a hormone called adrenaline, which gives you an energy boost to help you escape the danger. And as night falls, the pineal gland in your brain makes a hormone called melatonin, which causes you to feel sleepy and get ready to rest.

After all that wiring, you probably feel like doing that right now. So, relax, and take a deep breath ...

step 4

Set Up the Power Plant

ALL AROUND In order to operate, your cells, brain and every other part of your body require a steady supply of oxygen. And how do you obtain that? Yes, by breathing in that lovely oxygen-rich air that's all around you. So the next step is to add two lungs to draw air into your human, and then a heart and blood vessels to pump it round the body.

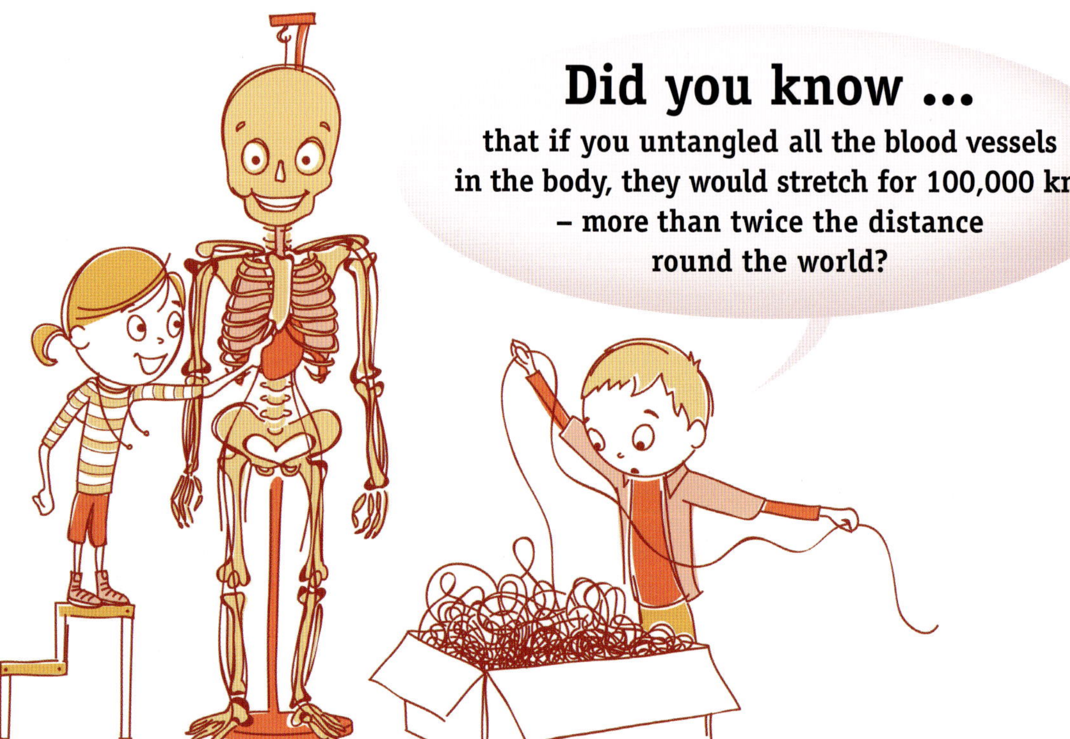

Did you know ...
that if you untangled all the blood vessels in the body, they would stretch for 100,000 km – more than twice the distance round the world?

AIR BAGS Carefully lift the lungs. Soft, spongy and moist, aren't they? Begin by attaching them to that bendy, ribbed tube that looks a bit like the pipe that sticks out of the back of a washing machine. It's called the windpipe, or trachea. Then slide the lungs and windpipe up into the rib cage so that the windpipe reaches the throat. Easy does it!

Make sure you have the lungs the right way round: the right-hand lung is bigger and has three sections (lobes), while the one on the left is smaller with just two. A wide muscle called the diaphragm slots under the lungs and helps keep them in place.

HAVE A HEART In the little space beside the smaller left lung, place the heart, that oval-shaped organ a bit bigger than your fist. Next, connect it to the major blood vessels – thick tubes known as arteries and slightly thinner ones called veins. The arteries and veins join smaller arteries and veins, which in turn connect with tiny blood vessels called capillaries. It's a bit like a road network with motorways, main roads and minor roads.

Some of the capillaries are much thinner than hairs, and there are a lot of them. How many? Ooh, about 300 million or so. Let's hope you didn't have any important appointments!

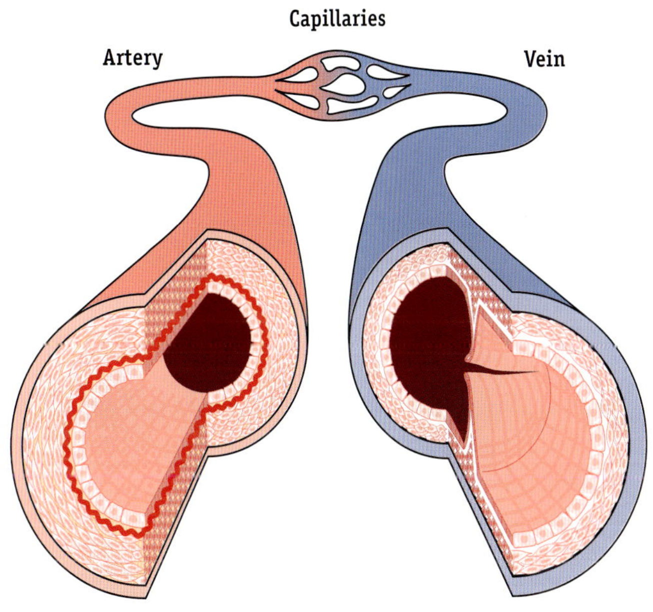

IN AND OUT ... As you breathe in (try it now, yourself), your brain directs your chest muscles to pull your ribs up and out, and your diaphragm to sink down. This expands the lungs and draws air in from outside the body. As you breathe out, the chest muscles let the ribs sink down again and the diaphragm moves upwards, pushing the air out again. In and out ... in and out ... in and out ...

THE TREE OF LIFE

Air enters the lungs through two major airways called the bronchi (singular: bronchus). Inside each lung, the bronchus joins smaller bronchi, which branch into narrower pipes called bronchioles. It's a bit like an upside down tree with hundreds of branches and thousands of twigs – in fact it's called the 'respiratory tree'.

Hanging at the end of the twigs, or bronchioles, are clusters of air sacs – like miniature bunches of grapes. These are called alveoli. When air reaches the alveoli, oxygen from the air passes into the surrounding blood vessels and is whisked off around the body, delivered to every part of you.

The lungs contain more than 300 million alveoli and 2,400 km of airways – roughly the distance from Paris to Moscow.

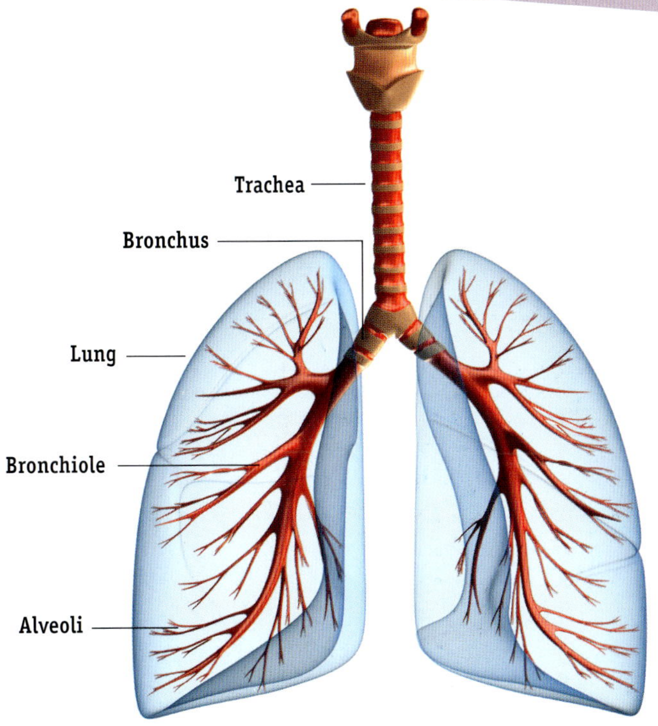

At the same time, unwanted gases from the blood (mainly carbon dioxide) are returned from the blood vessels to the alveoli and then travel back up the respiratory tree and out of the lungs – as you breathe out.

FASTER, FASTER!

Probably at this point you're nice and relaxed, and your breathing is steady, at a rate of about 15 breaths a minute. But once you put this book down and get back to lifting bones and hooking up organs – or do any other exercise – your muscles will have to work harder. And then you'll need more oxygen, and you'll breathe faster to get it. You don't have to think about this though – your brain takes care of everything, as it does most of the time.

Even if you decide to stop breathing, your brain won't let you. You can hold your breath for a minute or two, but your brain will soon take charge and force you to breathe again.

PUMPING! Your heart is a powerful pump that keeps blood moving constantly round your body. Lie still in a quiet place and put your hand on your chest. Can you feel your heart pumping? Yes? Phew, you're still alive then.

The left side of the heart sends oxygen-rich blood from the lungs to the rest of the body, while the right side pumps oxygen-poor blood from the body back to the lungs. Each side has an upper chamber called an atrium (plural: atria) and a lower chamber called a ventricle.

GET WITH THE BEAT

Blood enters the atria then valves open and let it fall into the ventricles. After those valves close, the heart muscles pump the blood out of another set of valves into the arteries. The sound of the valves opening and closing is your heartbeat.

While the oxygen-poor blood flows to the lungs, the oxygen-rich blood travels through the arteries to the capillaries. These are so thin that the oxygen can seep into the surrounding tissue. The deoxygenated blood then flows into the veins, which direct it back to the heart.

GO WITH THE FLOW

As well as oxygen, blood carries loads of other vital substances around your body. More than half of your blood is a clear, watery substance called plasma, which transports important nutrients as well as blood cells. Red blood cells give blood its colour, and convey oxygen and remove waste gases.

White blood cells are far fewer in number – there's only one for every 700 red cells – but vitally important too. They kill off unfriendly bacteria and viruses that might make you sick. The blood also contains cell fragments called platelets, which form a clot at the site of a cut to stop it bleeding and help it heal.

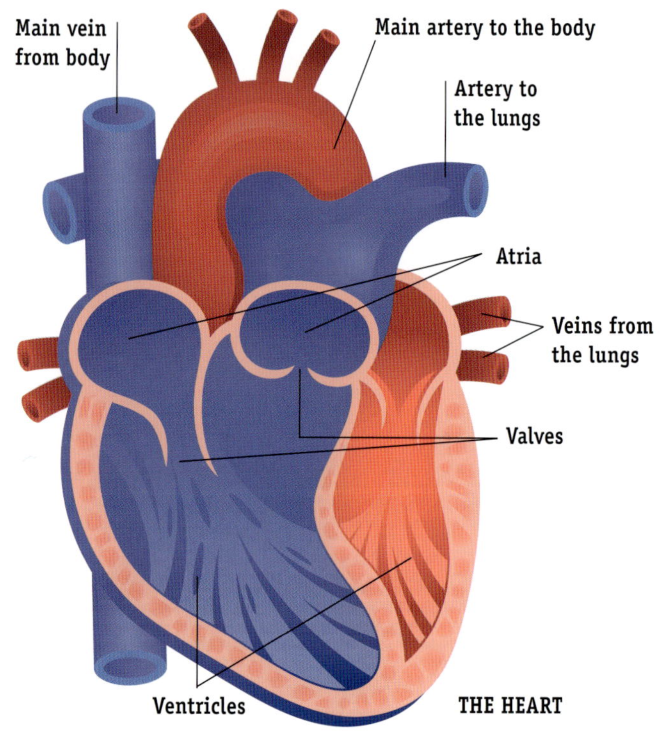

THE HEART

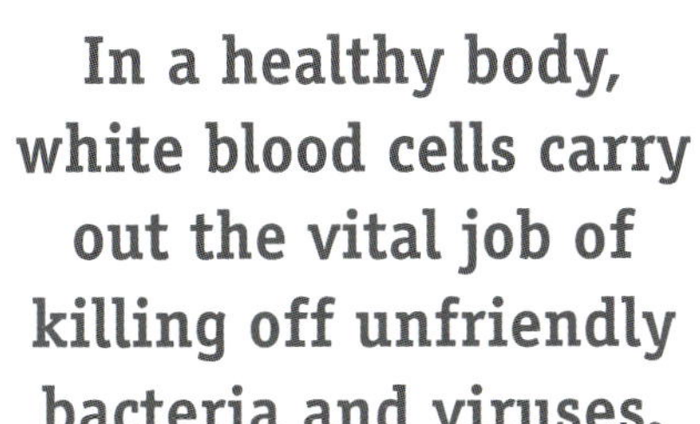

In a healthy body, white blood cells carry out the vital job of killing off unfriendly bacteria and viruses.

CALL FOR BACK UP

White blood cells also patrol another system that helps fight disease, the lymphatic system. It consists of a network of vessels that drain excess fluid from tissues. A small organ called the spleen, which sits under your lower left ribs, is part of this system; it creates extra germ-fighting white blood cells.

Strung along the lymphatic vessels like beads are nodes that filter out germs and other nasties. When you have an infection, they often swell up and you can feel them as lumps or 'swollen glands', as they are often called.

What, another whole system of vessels to install? Afraid so. After that, you're really going to need refuelling.

step 5

HOOK UP THE FUEL SYSTEM

ENERGY SOURCE

Body fuel? What's that, you might say? Well, it's not coal or steam, electricity or gas, but food of course. Eating is what gives you energy to run, jump, breathe and read this book, and your body has a whole set of parts, called the digestive system, dedicated to turning food into energy – as well as getting rid of what you don't need.

OPEN WIDE! Food enters the body through the mouth, and that's where you need to start connecting up the digestive system. Check that all the teeth are present and correct, because

they are essential for chopping up your food into small pieces.

As a young child, you have 20 baby or milk teeth, but, as you will have noticed, these gradually fall out, giving you that funny, gappy smile we all have between the ages of about six and ten. So cute! Luckily for us and our photo albums, our milk teeth are replaced by large, shiny adult teeth – eventually 32 in all.

Look in the mirror or feel around with your tongue and you'll see that there are three main kinds of teeth. The eight shovel-shaped ones in the middle at the front are called incisors. They chop food while the four pointy teeth on either side of them, called the canines, grip and rip it. The flatter, squarer teeth at the back – the molars – chew and grind.

Each tooth has a deep root that slots into the jaw and is protected by the gum. Above the gum, the tooth is covered in enamel – the hardest substance in a human.

MOUTH-WATERING!

As you chew your food, spit – known more correctly as saliva – makes it moist and soft. Saliva comes from glands under your tongue and at the back of your mouth, and it contains chemicals called enzymes that kill germs and start breaking down the food.

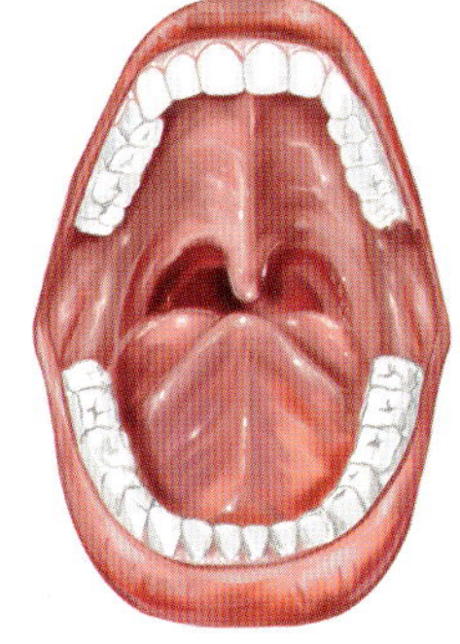

As soon as you see or smell food, your brain tells the glands to make more saliva in preparation for eating – your mouth waters, in other words. Always try not to dribble though.

HOLUS BOLUS As your teeth chop and chew, your tongue and cheek muscles shape the soggy food into a squishy ball called a bolus. Then the tongue rolls it to the back of your mouth, ready for swallowing.

The muscles in your digestive system are so strong that you can even eat upside down – although it's definitely not recommended!

NO CHOKE

The back of the mouth is connected to a long tube of muscle called the oesophagus. Slide this down into the rib cage, behind the windpipe. Next you need to put a lid on the windpipe so that your human doesn't choke when eating. This consists of a small flap of tissue called the epiglottis. As you swallow, it flips down over the top of the trachea and stops food going down your airways instead of the oesophagus. How cool is that?!

DOWN THE HATCH

Once headed in the right direction, your food doesn't just plummet down the oesophagus like a kid on a slide. Though gravity certainly lends a hand, throat muscles give the bolus a big shove to speed it on its way, then muscles around the oesophagus tighten one after another to keep it whooshing down the slippery, mucus-lined tunnel.

This muscle action, which continues all the way through your digestive system, is called peristalsis. It's so powerful that you can even swallow food when you are upside down. This is not the safest or neatest way to eat, though.

Stomach

CHYME OUT

Pass the bottom of the oesophagus through the hole in the diaphragm and attach it to the stomach. Shaped something like a fat banana, the stomach is the body's major food processor. Looking at the empty stomach, you may wonder how it holds those humungous meals you eat. Fortunately, it is lined with folds and covered with stretchy muscles, which allow it to expand, making the space inside up to 24 times bigger than when the stomach is empty.

The oesophagus delivers the bolus to the stomach in seconds roughly the time it took you to read this sentence. Using powerful muscle contractions, the stomach then pummels the bolus while releasing acidic juices that break the food down further. After a few hours, the result is a mushy goo called chyme.

STRONG ACID

The acids in your stomach are strong enough to strip paint off a wall or dissolve soft metals. Luckily, thick mucus protects your stomach lining.

NO THANKS!

Of course, occasionally your stomach detects so many bad bacteria in food – for example, in food that has gone off – that it rejects it. Peristalsis then goes into reverse and sends the food flying back up the oesophagus, so you can vomit it out. Yuck!

WHERE THE ACTION IS

The lower end of the stomach joins to the top of a long tube called the small intestine. Be careful when attaching this, as it's more than 5 m long and has to be folded dozens of times to fit into the space under the stomach. Don't get in a tangle!

Above the stomach, place the large organ called the liver and attach it to the little bag-like gall bladder. Then slot the long, crinkly pancreas under the stomach. The liver, gall bladder and pancreas all join to the top part of the small intestine, the duodenum, the scene of some intensive digestive action.

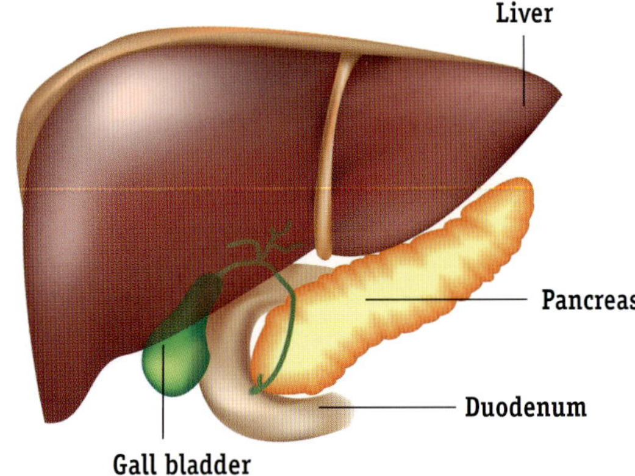

ENERGY TRANSFER

The biggest organ inside your body, the liver produces a green liquid called bile, which is stored in the gall bladder and squirted into the duodenum as food passes through. Bile breaks down fats and boosts digestion. The pancreas also supplies fluids that aid digestion. In addition, it produces a vital hormone called insulin that controls blood sugar levels.

Multi-Tasking

Making bile is just one of roughly 500 tasks handled by the amazing liver. Packed with blood vessels, it removes germs from the blood, controls the flow of nutrients to the body, regulates hormones, and stores vitamins and minerals. All at once, all day and every day. Pretty impressive, huh?

Swallowed air and gases from digestion are released as wind. Most people emit about 1 litre of gas a day, either quietly or with accompanying noises!

As the chyme is pushed slowly along the small intestine over six or so hours, it is finally broken down into nutrients that the body can absorb. These pass through the wrinkly wall of the intestine and into the bloodstream.

DOWN TO THE BOTTOM Connect the end of the small intestine to the large intestine – a thicker tube about 1.5 m long. It runs back up the right-hand side of the abdomen, across the top of the small intestine and then down the left side to the bottom of the pelvis.

Over several hours, the large intestine absorbs water and salts from the remaining food waste and transfers them to the blood. Trillions of friendly bacteria – ten times as many as there are cells in your body – help out.

WAY OUT Finally, a few times a day, muscles in the intestines push the remaining semisolid waste matter – poo or, more correctly, faeces – into the last part of the intestine, the rectum. And there it remains until you take your next toilet break.

step 6

Place the Plumbing

Sloshing about

Of course, it's not just solid waste you need to get rid of regularly. Water makes up more than half of a human's weight and is a vital component of numerous body functions. So there's going to be a lot of it sloshing about inside your human. You'd better get a decent plumbing system in place then.

By weight, your brain consists of 75 per cent water and your lungs almost 90 per cent water.

Body of water

Your cells are full of water, and water makes up most of the liquids that carry nutrients around your body – including your blood. Water also moistens tissues, lubricates muscles and joints, improves digestion, flushes out toxins, and helps regulate fat and control body temperature. Wow!

So you need a steady supply of fresh water to keep everything in tip-top condition – roughly 2.5 litres a day, and more if you are doing lots of sweaty exercise. About half the water will come from food, but the other half needs to be in the form of liquids, preferably plain, simple water.

Good drainage

Water enters your body through the digestive system and is absorbed into the bloodstream. As fresh water comes in, used water, along with toxic body wastes, winds its way out, via a series of filters, tanks and pipes called the urinary system. This includes two bean-shaped, fist-sized organs called the

Um, who did that?

kidneys, which control water levels in the body and extract waste from the blood.

Position the kidneys at the back of your human, one on each side of the spine under the lower ribs and just above the hips, and connect them to the major blood vessels. Next, join the kidneys to the two long drainage tubes, the ureters, and hook these up to the bag-like bladder, which sits inside the bottom of the pelvis.

Drink Up!

Feeling thirsty? That's your brain telling you that you need more water. If you don't respond, your body will start drawing water from body cells and muscles and you won't feel so well. This is called dehydration. And if you don't consume any water at all, you won't survive more than a few days. Time for a drink?

WATER FILTERS

Blood passes steadily through the kidneys along a complex network of thin blood vessels and tiny filters called nephrons – there are more than a million of these in each kidney! The nephrons extract excess water and small amounts of waste chemicals. These combine as a yellowish liquid called urine, which trickles into the ureters.

The kidneys adjust the flow and concentration of urine according to the amount of water you have taken in. If you haven't had enough and are slightly dehydrated, your urine will contain less water, turning it a darker yellow. That's a reminder to fill your glass and drink up!

WHEN YOU GOTTA GO

Muscles in the ureters repeatedly contract (just as they do in the oesophagus) and push urine down

The empty bladder is the size of a plum.

The full bladder is the size of a grapefruit.

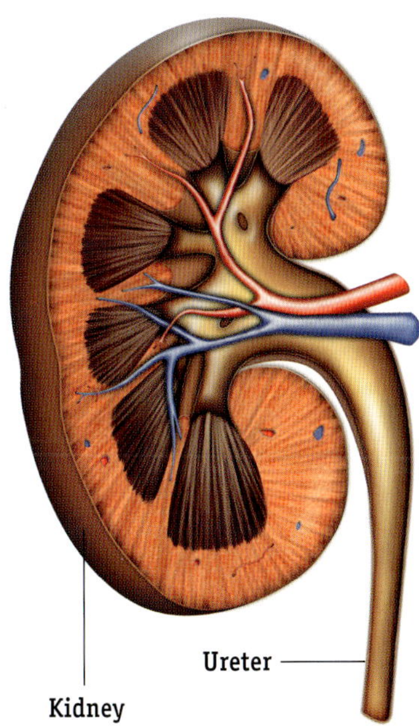

to the bladder. This flexible bag is about the size of a plum when empty, but can expand to about the size of a grapefruit as it fills.

Once there's half a cup or so of urine in your bladder, stretch receptors alert the brain, which starts advising you that you will soon need to go to the toilet. You might ignore these signals for a while, but once the bladder level is up to a cup or so they'll start getting stronger and stronger till you're squirming and hopping around and just *have* to go!

PIPED OUT An opening at the bottom of the bladder leads to your water outlet, a thin tube called the urethra. Normally, the opening from the bladder to the urethra is shut tight by a ring of muscles, or sphincter. But when you are ready to go to the toilet, you can release these muscles and let the waste water flow out. Aaah ...

MESSY! Of course, there was a time when you couldn't do that and it was all a lot messier – when you were a baby. Newborns have no idea how to control their bladder or rectum muscles and have to gradually learn how to do it. Thank goodness for nappies.

Your kidneys filter about 150 litres of blood every day – equivalent to processing all your blood 30 times!

Reinforce and Strengthen

MUSCLE POWER

Now that you've got all the major components in place, you can start wrapping the body in muscles. These will support and protect the bones and organs, and get your human moving!

INSIDE AND OUT Most of your organs have muscles that help them function – the muscles that pump the heart, push food along the intestines, and so on. The heart muscles are called cardiac muscles and the other organ muscles are known as smooth muscles. All are controlled by your brain without you even thinking about it. They work automatically, in other words.

In contrast, the muscles that cover your bones and organs – the skeletal muscles – work when you decide to do something, like bend, jump, do a cartwheel or stand on your head.

If you use a muscle a lot, the fibres inside thicken and the muscle grows larger.

TIE THEM ON

Skeletal muscles cover a human from top to toe and there are about 650 of them in all. So strapping them on is going to keep you pretty busy. Most stretch from one end of a bone across its surface to join with another bone. Use the cord-like extensions at the ends of the muscles – called tendons – to attach them. Tendons can be quite long. For example, five long ones link the fingers to muscles in the forearm, and another five connect the toes to the lower leg muscles.

Some muscles are large, like those that support the back, and the quadriceps at the front of the thigh. Others are small and tricky to handle. Yes, you guessed it, those hands and feet are going to be hard work again! Nearly 40 muscles connect the wrist, fingers and thumb alone.

MOVE IT!

When you decide to move, your brain tells the appropriate muscles to contract, or tighten. This pulls the bones in one direction. Releasing the contraction lets the bones move back again.

WORKING TOGETHER

Often muscles work in pairs. To bend your fist up towards your shoulder, for example, you have to tighten the large muscle at the front of your upper arm, the biceps brachii, while relaxing the muscle at the back of the upper arm, the triceps brachii. And to let your fist down again and straighten your arm, you relax the biceps while contracting the triceps. Try it out, and get your human to do it too. Practice makes perfect!

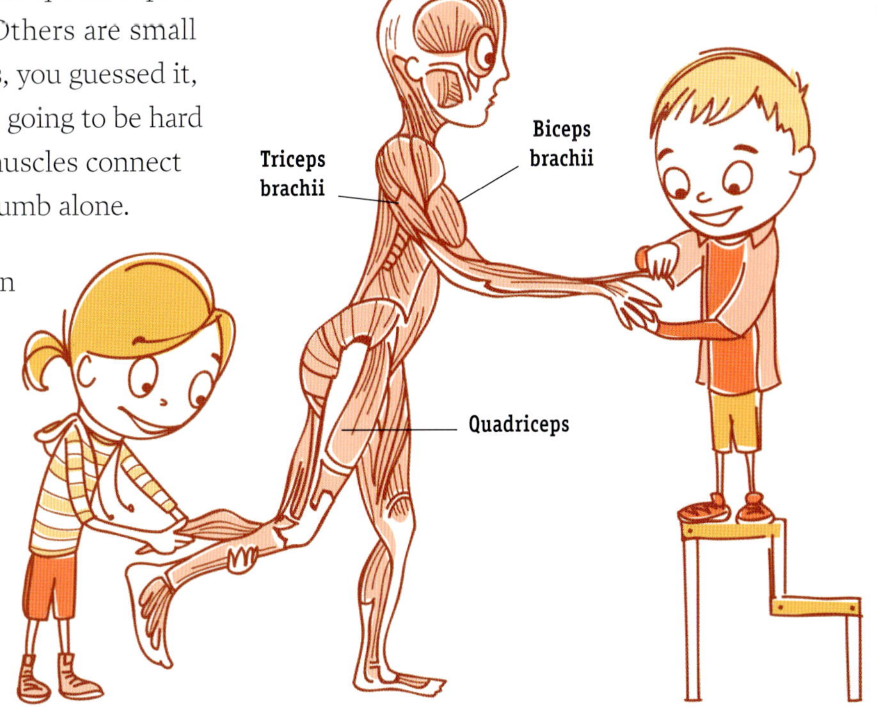

STEP BY STEP

Most movements are much more complicated than that, though. Take walking, for instance. It seems easy, doesn't it – just one step in front of the other? But that's because you've had plenty of practice.

Walking actually involves about 200 muscles and many complex movements. First the hip muscles on one side pull that leg up off the ground and swing it forward, while the muscles in the other leg tighten to support the full weight of the body. As the first leg swings forward, its thigh muscles help straighten it and the shin and foot muscles lift the foot up off the ground.

Then, as the foot lands, the calf and the long hamstring muscles at the back of the other leg lift the heel, and the muscles in the ball of that foot push upwards as the hip muscles start the next step.

LOTS TO LEARN

Gosh! If you had to think it through like that every time you made a step, you'd probably never get anywhere – or even *want* to go anywhere. But fortunately you spent months mastering all this when you were a baby and toddler – wobbling around, crashing into things, falling over and crying – and now you do it without thinking. Your human, however, still has a lot to learn.

You probably take about 10,000 steps a day.

Mini Movements

Most other body movements are similarly complicated, even the littlest ones. There are more than 30 different muscles in the face, for example, and at least 12 need to work together just to get you to smile. Come on, do it now!

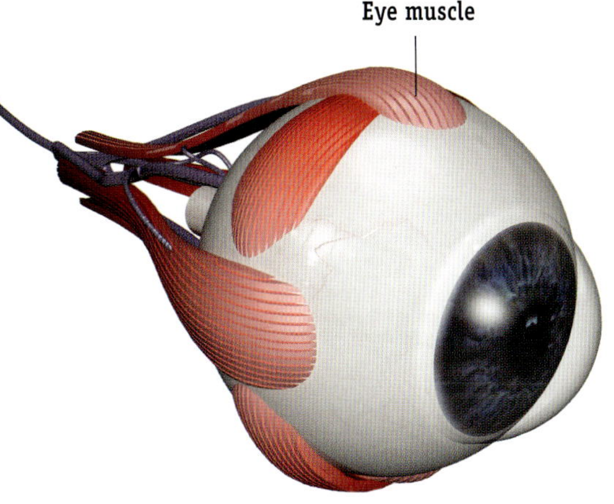

Some of these little muscles have to work really hard. For instance, several small ones pull your eyelids up and down to spread tears across the eyes and keep them moist and clean – this is called blinking. They do this about 10 times a minute – or 14,400 times a day! In fact, in an average lifetime, a human will blink about 400 million times. Phew! It's just as well *they* get a rest at night.

Even more hard-working are the six straplike muscles that make your eyes move. Think how busy they are now, as you follow these words back and forth across the page!

It takes at least 12 different facial muscles to let you smile.

Test of Nerve

Doctors sometimes whack people just below the knee with a hammer when they are sitting down. Not to punish them or make them pay their bills but to test their nerve and muscle function. In a healthy patient, the blow will send a signal to the spinal cord to tighten the thigh muscle, causing the leg to kick upwards. If this doesn't happen, it may be a sign of nerve damage.

step 8

Select Finishes and Features

SUITS YOU By now that human of yours is probably raring to get out and about. But before that happens, you need to seal everything with a nice suit of skin and add further protection in the form of nails and hair.

The skin is the body's biggest organ and it is also surprisingly heavy – a full adult suit weighs about 5 kg, so take care when lifting it. The skin should cover the whole surface of your human, except for openings such as the mouth and eyes, of course.

COLOUR AND PATTERNS Skin comes in several colours, and the precise shade varies according to the amount of melanin in the skin. Melanin is a pigment that absorbs harmful rays from the sun. Generally, people who live in hot parts of the world have more melanin and therefore darker skin.

SCORCHING!

Exposing your skin to the sun increases the amount of melanin in your skin, making it darker or suntanned. But if you get too much sun, you may end up sunburned – ouch! – and cause long-term damage to your skin.

Dead skin constantly flakes off your body. You lose tens of thousands of flakes every minute and over a lifetime can shed 50 kg of skin – the average weight of a 14-year-old!

Paler skins sometimes also have distinctive patterns of marks called freckles. These are concentrated spots of melanin. Often they disappear as you get older.

IDENTIFYING MARKS

Fit the skin over the muscles and smooth it out. Don't worry if there are a few creases and folds at the joints. Everyone has those, even babies.

You'll notice that the pads on the fingers and toes have swirly patterns of ridges and grooves. These will help your human grip things. They're also a handy means of identification, as no two people have the same patterns or prints.

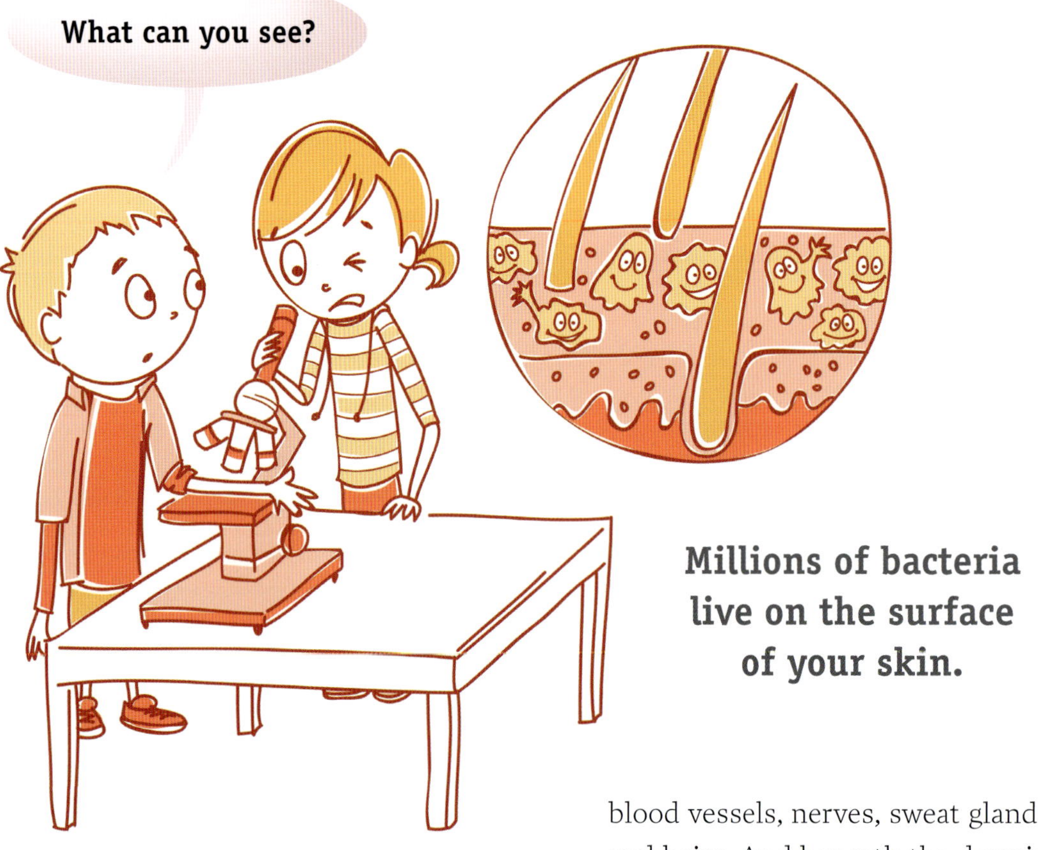

Millions of bacteria live on the surface of your skin.

DEAD TOUGH It's quite thick in places, that suit of skin, isn't it? Especially on the palms of the hands and the soles of the feet. And there's more to it than you might think. The thin outer layer, or epidermis, is a busy factory, constantly producing millions of skin cells. These form at the bottom of the layer and are steadily pushed upwards. By the time they reach the surface, they are dead – but tough.

Underneath the epidermis is a thicker layer called the dermis, which is threaded with thousands of tiny blood vessels, nerves, sweat glands, and hairs. And beneath the dermis is a layer of squishy fat.

SHOCK PROTECTION Dark or light, suntanned or freckled, skin does an amazing job of protecting us. It's not only a sunscreen but also waterproof, washable and tough – it can resist heavy blows and you can twist and pull it (not too hard though!) without causing lasting damage. Even when skin is cut through, it heals remarkably quickly.

DUST COVER Skin also keeps out bacteria that might interfere with the body's processes or make you

sick. Not that your skin is a germ-free zone. In fact, millions of bacteria live on its outer surface all the time – at least 10 million in every square centimetre! Eek!

Don't panic, though. Most are friendly bacteria that help keep other, more dangerous germs away. You never knew you had so many friends, did you?

TEMPERATURE CONTROL As well as sensing heat and cold, skin helps control your body's temperature. Feeling hot? As soon as you do, the blood vessels in your skin will widen to let heat out and the sweat glands will release sweat (99 per cent water), which evaporates from the surface of the skin, cooling it down.

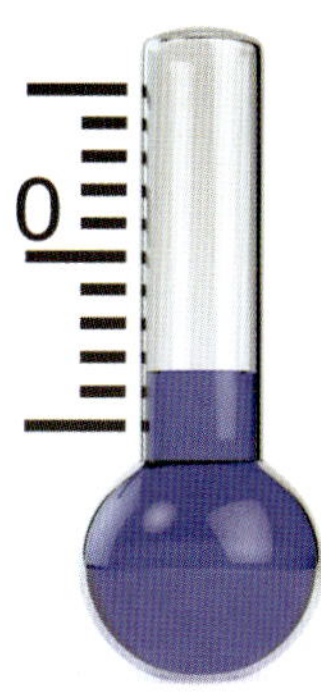

When you are cold your body makes your muscles move to generate heat – you shiver – and blood vessels in the skin narrow to keep heat in. Hairs also tend to stand on end, creating what we call goosebumps. Brr!

ITCHY AND SCRATCHY Sensitive stuff, your skin feels all sorts of things – pleasant stroking, playful tickling, occasional itching. And when you've got an itch, you've got to be able to scratch, and the best way to do that is with your fingernails. Nails aren't just for scratching, though. They protect the ends of your fingers and toes, and help you pick up tiny objects.

A pocket under the skin at the bottom of each nail constantly produces new cells. Like skin cells, by the time these nail cells see the light of day they are dead and hard – completely solid in this case. Nails grow at a rate of about 4 cm a year, so they need regular cutting. But no biting now!

Nails grow faster on the hand you use more and its middle fingernail grows fastest of all. No one knows why.

Crowning Glory

There will be hair growing all over your human's body, but it will be thickest on the head. How is it? Dark or blonde? Dense and wavy, or fine and straight? Really cool, or just a bit weird? Not to worry, if you feel it doesn't suit, you can always get your scissors, gel and hairdryer out and restyle it. You can chop it, curl it, flatten it or make it stick up straight, even dye it if you like.

Hair, Hair

It's amazing stuff, hair. But what's it for (aside from making you look even more stylish) and what's it made of? Well, the hair on your head provides extra sun protection for the most exposed and vital part of your body and helps keep heat in.

Like skin and nails, hair forms from dead cells. Hair cells form at the bottom of narrow pockets in the skin, called follicles, and are pushed upwards by new cells, forming a long strand. Glands attached to the follicle coat the growing hair in oil, or sebum, to make it bendy and soft.

Colour and Style

You might dye your hair green or purple, but your natural colour is set by your genes, those detailed instructions stored in your DNA, and it's created by melanin, the substance

Follicular Fall Out

Check out your dad, uncle or any other older guy nearby. Has his hair gone grey or even white? Is it thinning a bit, or even missing completely? In later life, follicles stop producing melanin and hair loses its colour. And men especially start to lose hair. How much they lose, and where and when, depends on their genes.

Head hair grows about 1 cm a month. You lose up to 100 hairs a day, but fortunately you've got about 100,000.

that also gives skin its colour. The thickness and style of your hair depend on your follicles. The wider they are, the thicker your hair. Round follicles produce straight hair, oval follicles make wavy hair, and narrow follicles create curly hair.

USEFUL SPROUTS

Special hairs sprout in other places too. Thick hairs grow inside the nose to catch germs and dust. Eyelashes line eyelids to keep dirt out of the eyes. And men have facial hair they can grow into funny-looking moustaches and beards.

Male or female, you have plenty of hair. But nothing like enough to keep you completely warm. So before your human starts getting cold, or just embarrassed, it's time to select a set of clothes – something stylish, of course.

step 9

Test and Train

ONLY HUMAN

Your human is almost complete and, if all has gone to plan, will look and move much like you. And soon, with a little help, it will learn to do all you can do – maybe more!

A human can do things that few or no other creatures can do. Check whether your human can master the following, for example. Walking on two legs? That seems to be going well. Touching the thumb to the middle finger on the same hand – no problem? You've definitely got a human then, as, although this seems ridiculously simple, no other animal can manage it.

LAUGHTER AND TEARS

How about laughing? No other creatures laugh as we do. Tell your human a joke, do a funny dance, or try tickling it. Did you get a laugh, a chuckle or even a titter? Excellent.

As with laughter, so with tears. While other animals mourn and make sad noises, none cry like humans. When we are very sad, or especially happy, tears – which are produced constantly by glands in our eyes to keep them moist – overflow and stream down our face.

WHAT'S THE MATTER?

As well as laughing and crying, humans have other ways of expressing their emotions. We might

OK, I think that's enough!

use hand gestures, for example – waving a fist to express anger or folding the arms across the chest to show defiance.

And we employ all those little muscles in the face to make a wide range of expressions. Raised eyebrows show surprise, a frown displays anger or concern, wrinkling the nose expresses disgust. Crossing your eyes and sticking out your tongue means you've gone mad (possibly). Go on, teach your human to make faces – it's a useful skill!

PUZZLE AND PONDER Gradually, your human will start thinking for itself. It will begin to understand causes and effects and work out how things happen. And it will start to remember things.

Memory is a vital brain function that helps us understand the world and learn how to interact with it. The human brain stores two main types of memories: short-term and long-term.

Short-term memories are images and information that we need to deal with what we are doing now and in the immediate future – where you put your school bag, for example. Most are forgotten soon after. Long-term memories are impressions and facts that stay with us, either because we experienced them repeatedly or they were especially significant to us. Like your first thrilling ride on a rollercoaster – unforgettable!

SPEAK UP The combination of thought processes and memory will certainly make your human better at board games. And it will help it learn a host of other new skills. One, no doubt, will be talking – another thing only humans can do.

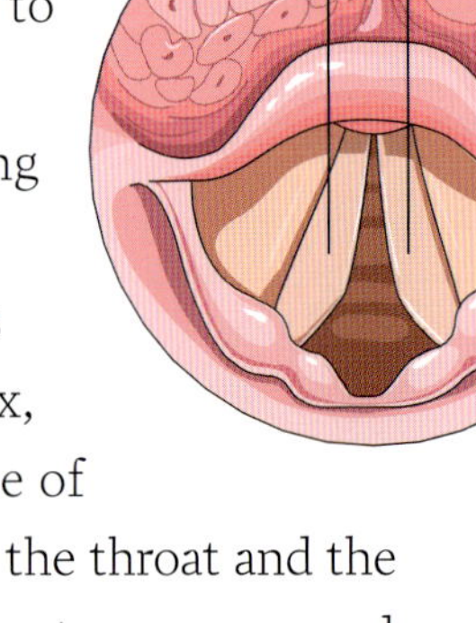

When you decide to speak, your brain tells your breathing muscles to push air from the lungs through the larynx, or voicebox, a tube of cartilage between the throat and the windpipe. This creates a raw sound. At the same time, your brain directs other muscles to open and close your vocal cords – two membranes at the top of the larynx – to vary the pitch of the sound. Try it now: make a high then a low sound.

SING OUT Meanwhile, other muscles move your mouth, lips and tongue to make the specific sounds we associate with letters and words. It's a tricky business and it took you many months to learn it, so be patient with your human! After that you can move on to singing!

PATHWAYS Once that brain gets going, there's no end to what your human will master. By repeating actions and thoughts many times, a human

Babies sleep for up to 18 hours a day, children need about 10 or 11 hours' sleep. Adults can usually make do with 8, though older people might sleep only 5 or 6 hours a night.

strengthens connections or pathways in the brain that eventually enable it to do things almost automatically, such as read, play a musical instrument, speak another language or juggle flaming torches without setting itself on fire.

RECHARGE Like all of us, however, your human will need to sleep regularly. Exactly why humans sleep for so long each day – we snooze away about one-third of our lives – is not fully understood. But it clearly allows the muscles and brain to recover from the day's activities.

Even when you're asleep though, your brain is still active, keeping you breathing and, every so often, getting you to change position. During periods of deep sleep, that's about all it does. But during lighter sleep – known as REM (rapid eye movement) sleep – it's up to all sorts of mischief, concocting weird dreams and occasionally – woo! – scary nightmares. It's thought that dreams may be a way for the brain to sort through and make sense of things that have happened to you. But then few dreams make sense at all, so go figure!

AUTO PILOT

It won't be long before your human can do almost everything by itself – tie its own shoelaces, help you with your homework, thrash you at table tennis or take out the rubbish. Eventually, it might even go its own way and make other friends, which could be a little sad for you (sob!). And at some point it might decide to make humans of its own.

Of course in real life, humans don't arrive in kits to be pieced together bit by bit. The reality is far more amazing.

YOU IN MINIATURE

Remember that single cell that started it all – that started you? (If not, have a quick look back at page 9.) It formed from two half cells, one half provided by your mother and one half by your father. Inside your mother, in an organ above the bladder called the uterus or womb, that one cell divided and divided, making millions of cells. After a few weeks, these formed tissues and skin, which then became a tiny human form called an embryo – you!

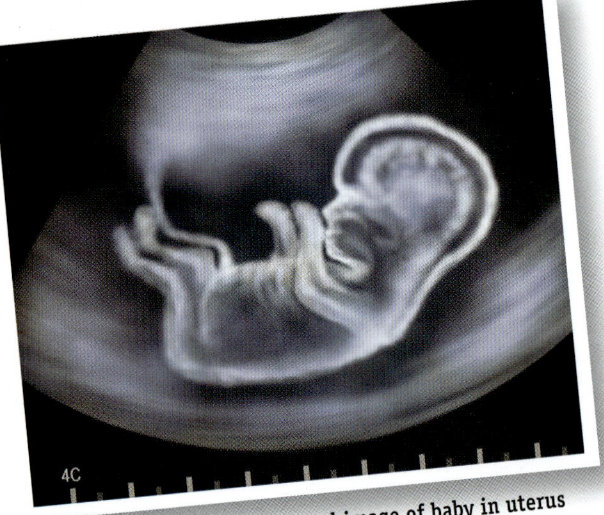

Ultrasound image of baby in uterus

After two months, you were still only about the size of a walnut, but you already had all your main parts and organs, and doctors started calling you a foetus (though your family no doubt had cuter names for you). Sheltered and nurtured by your mum, you grew rapidly over another seven months and then – cue drumroll and fanfare! – you were born. A momentous day!

GETTING THE HANG OF IT

For the first few months, you could hardly do anything for yourself. Your family fed you, changed you, helped you sit up, showed you how to walk and talk – a bit like you've been doing with *your* human. But you got the hang of it all and soon you were toddling around, babbling away at anyone and everything. And after a while people could even understand what you were saying.

LOTS TO LEARN

Later you learned to play games, make things, write and read. And here you are now, using those skills to read this book, make a human and find out about your body.

Like your new human, you've still got lots to learn. And your body will go on changing: you'll grow bigger, older and – of course! – wiser. But already, having put a human together, you'll have an excellent understanding of how a body works and what it can do. And by now, at least, you'll know this for sure – you're an absolute marvel, a wonder, a miraculous creature. Make the most of it!

step 10

Caring for a Human

HANDY HINTS Your human will eventually look after itself pretty well, just as your own body does. But to keep it in tip-top shape, make sure you provide healthy food, plenty of rest and exercise, and regular maintenance.

For best results, a human needs not just any old fuel but foods that are rich in nutrients, vitamins and minerals, such as fresh fruit and vegetables. Sugary and fatty foods should be given only in moderation. Fill up regularly with water, too.

MAINTENANCE AND CLEANING Make sure your human has plenty of sleep. If not, its brain and body systems will work less efficiently; memory lapses, mistakes and accidents will occur; and terrifying tantrums will be far more likely.

Wash daily to limit the spread of unfriendly bacteria and brush the teeth twice a day to prevent decay. Exercise is also essential to keep all parts running smoothly and limit the build-up of body fat. So, don't just sit there: run, jump, dance, climb, cycle, bounce on a trampoline. Find out what a human can do!

TROUBLESHOOTING No matter how much you prepare and protect, polish and pamper, things will occasionally go wrong – accidents *will* happen. All humans get hurt now and again, but fortunately the body can deal with most minor scrapes.

I didn't realise a human needed so much food!

Your human will need at least 500 kg of food each year (the weight of ten 14-year-olds). Not cheap to keep!

A heavy bump might make blood vessels under the skin bleed, forming a painful bruise, but this will soon fix itself without any treatment. Grazes and small cuts will also heal quickly, as first platelets clot the blood to form a scab and then new skin generates.

Though white blood cells are constantly on the alert for bacteria and viruses, illnesses may strike now and again. However, the body should deal with common infections such as stomach upsets and colds. Simply provide plenty of rest and lots to drink.

PRECAUTIONS

In the early stages, medical checkups are recommended to make sure everything is in working order. Humans can be given injections called vaccinations to protect them against a number of serious diseases. You should also see a dentist at regular intervals to check that the teeth are growing properly and fix any problems.

Viruses are tiny particles that invade cells and use them to multiply. They damage cells and cause illnesses.

ESSENTIAL REPAIRS

If a problem seems more serious, contact a doctor for treatment and repairs. Luckily, scientists have developed a wide range of medicines to fight illnesses, including antibiotics. These destroy dangerous germs that could otherwise kill people.

If your doctor isn't certain of the cause of a problem, he or she will order tests. Blood tests examine a sample of blood to see what kinds of bacteria or viruses are present. An X-ray can peer through flesh to photograph bones and organs, and other imaging systems like ultrasounds and MRI scans can create more detailed pictures of our insides. Tiny cameras can even film inside the oesophagus or intestines. Using all this information, a doctor can fix most problems.

EMERGENCIES

Occasionally, though, your human may need more urgent or major repairs. A long or deep cut may need to be stitched to permit healing. A broken bone usually has to be set in place with a plaster cast, though the super-efficient body will do the rest. First blood will fill the break, then cartilage will grow there and after six weeks or so new bone will have taken its place. Phenomenal!

In some cases, a doctor may have to open a human up to fix something. Fortunately, the wonders of modern anaesthetics mean that the human won't feel a thing and can often sleep through the whole procedure.

SPARE PARTS

And if a body part can't be repaired, fear not. Many parts can now be replaced. Creaky hip and knee joints are routinely swapped for shiny metal or plastic ones. Artificial limbs can replace damaged arms and legs. Major organs, including the liver, kidneys and even the heart, can be transplanted from other humans.

LIFETIME WARRANTY

If the above instructions are followed closely, a human body should provide many decades of fun and pleasure. Who knows what amazing things yours will do?

Of course, some body parts will eventually wear out and, ultimately, it will cease functioning altogether. But look after it well – feed it, groom it, care for it and love it – and it *will* last a lifetime. Guaranteed.

AMAZING FACTS

All of the following numbers are averages.

Standard Model

Average adult height: **175 cm**

Average adult weight: **72 kg**

Cells

Number of cells in human body: **75 trillion**

Number of new cells produced each day: **300 billion**

Number of chromosomes in each cell: **46**

Skeleton

Number of bones: **206**

Number of joints: **approximately 400**

Number of bones in hands and feet: **106**

Number of bones in skull: **28**

Control Centre

Length of main nerve vessels: **70 km**

Speed of messages from nerves to brain: **up to 360 kilometres per hour**

Number of light sensors in each eye: **125 million**

Number of smells a human can distinguish: **10,000**

Number of tastebuds on tongue: **10,000**

Blood Supply

Length of all blood vessels: **100,000 km**

Number of capillaries: **300 million**

Lifespan of a red blood cell: **4 months**

Time for a blood cell to circle the body: **60 seconds**

Red blood cells per litre of blood: **4 trillion**

Volume of blood (child): **5 litres**

Volume of blood (adult): **6 litres**

Power Plant

Number of breaths each day: **23,000**

Number of heartbeats each day (adult): **100,000**

Number of heartbeats each day (child): **130,000**

Length of airways in lungs: **2400 km**

Surface area of airways in lungs: **70 square metres**

Speed of a sneeze: **60–100 kilometres per hour** (fastest ever recorded is 167 kilometres per hour)

Fuel System

Length of digestive system: **9 m**

Length of small intestine: **5–6 m**

Amount of saliva produced each day: **1 litre**

Time taken to digest a meal: **1–3 days**

Plumbing

Percentage of body weight that is water: **50–60%**

Percentage of brain that is water: **75%**

Percentage of lungs that is water: **90%**

Volume of blood filtered by kidneys each day: **150 litres**

Length of each ureter: **30 cm**

Muscles

Number of skeletal muscles: **approximately 650**

Number of muscles in hand: **40**

Number of muscles in tongue: **16**

Number of muscles involved in taking one step: **200**

Number of times eyes blink each day: **14,400**

Number of times eyes blink in a lifetime: **400 million**

Number of changes of position when asleep in one night: **45**

Skin and Hair

Weight of skin: **5 kg**

Area covered by skin: **1.6–2 square metres**

Volume of skin flakes shed in a lifetime: **50 kg**

Number of hairs on head: **100,000**

Lifespan of a hair: **3–7 years**

Hairs lost each day: **60–100**

Maintenance

Water required each year: **at least 900 litres**

Food required each year: **500 kg**

INDEX

Published by
Weldon Owen Limited
Northburgh House, 10 Northburgh Street
London EC1V 0AT, UK

weldonowenpublishing.com

Managing Director Sarah Odedina
Editorial Director Russell McLean
Sales Director Laurence Richard
US Sales Director Ellen Towell

Concept and Project Manager Ariana Klepac
Text Scott Forbes
Designer Mark Thacker, Big Cat Design
Picture Researcher Ariana Klepac
Consultant Jack Challoner
Illustrator Jean Camden, Hackett Films
Indexer Trevor Matthews

ISBN 978-1-74252-322-4

Printed and bound in China by 1010 Printing Int Ltd.

The paper used in the manufacture of this book is sourced from wood grown in sustainable forests. It complies with the Environmental Management System Standard ISO 14001:2004

A WELDON OWEN PRODUCTION

PICTURE CREDITS

JEAN CAMDEN, HACKETT FILMS: COVER, PAGES: 1, 3, 4 (TOP LEFT), 6, 8 (RIGHT), 9 (TOP), 10 (TOP LEFT, BOTTOM LEFT), 11 (BOTTOM), 12 (BOTTOM RIGHT), 13 (TOP RIGHT), 14 (TOP RIGHT), 15, 16 (BOTTOM), 17 (TOP), 19 (BOTTOM), 20 (TOP), 21 (TOP RIGHT), 22 (TOP), 23 (BOTTOM), 24 (BOTTOM), 26 (BOTTOM), 28 (BOTTOM), 29 (TOP RIGHT), 30 (TOP RIGHT), 31 (LEFT), 32 (BOTTOM RIGHT), 33 (TOP RIGHT), 34 (TOP), 35 (TOP), 36–37 (BOTTOM), 39, 40 (BOTTOM), 41 (BOTTOM), 42 (LEFT), 43 (BOTTOM), 44 (TOP), 45 (BOTTOM LEFT), 46 (TOP), 47 (BOTTOM), 48 (TOP), 50 (TOP), 51 (RIGHT), 53 (TOP, BOTTOM LEFT), 54 (BOTTOM), 55 (TOP), 56 (TOP), 57 (BOTTOM), 59 (TOP), 60 (LEFT), 61 (BOTTOM)

SHUTTERSTOCK: ALL OTHER IMAGES

For Ruari, Jamie, Lara, Hayden, Minnie Bo, Mal, Max, Frankie, Vinnie and Lola

Scott Forbes is a writer and editor who has worked in publishing in the UK and Australia for more than 20 years. He is the author of *The Reader's Digest Children's Atlas of the World* and *How to Make a Planet* and has contributed to numerous other natural history, science, travel and reference books.

Consultant **Jack Challoner** is a physicist and educator who is passionate about 'explaining science'. He is the author of many notable science books for both children and adults, he worked on the London Science Museum's flagship interactive gallery *LaunchPad*, and he has also developed television shows for BBC Scotland.

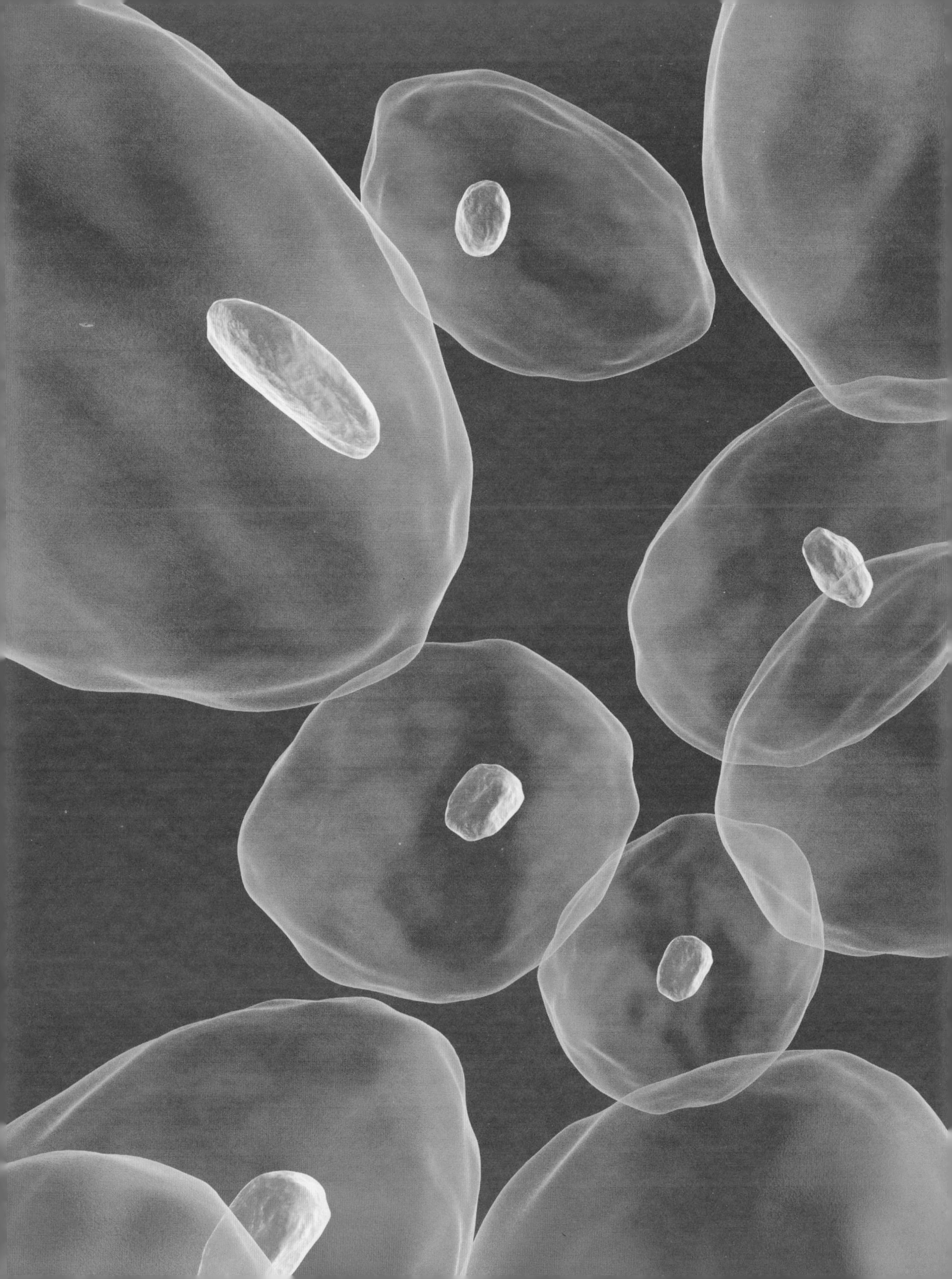